I0477974

The Trending Code

Charlie Collins

Author and Developer: Charlie Collins
Editor: Amy Collins
Website: www.trendingcodes.com

Copyright © 2018 by FairTran, LLC.

Published by FairTran, LLC.

Contents

Introduction

One of the most difficult things to do as a data analyst is to analyze trends and assemble comprehensive forecast models. Sure, you can run group queries and create a graph that you can visually process, and you can easily compare that graph with a handful of other graphs. But can you compare that graph with thousands of other graphs simultaneously over an indefinite period of time? Not likely. At least until now.

Traditional data analysis and reporting provides useful and valuable information like comparing current data to information from the prior year or years. However, it becomes increasingly difficult to compare today's trend (the cumulative upturns and downturns over a given period of time) to the trend of the prior year or years. We can know where we are currently, and we can even look to graphs to have an idea of where we are going, but how can we use a computer to analyze the trend or run reports off of the trend? How can we find out the last time that we experienced the current trend?

The trending code solves this problem by easily and efficiently allowing you to compare past data trends to create future projections. The code contains all of the trending data for a particular period of time, and this code can be queried to create reports, comparisons, and forecasts. The code is easy to read by the computer and by humans and can be used in any situation that involves periodic data - stock market research, banks, businesses, schools, churches, government agencies, sports, and on and on.

With the trending code, one five digit number gives you a wealth of information. With this one number, you can compare it to trending codes of other sectors. For example you could compare stocks and answer questions like, when was the last time the trending code for stock XYZ and stock ABC was the same as today? What was the trending code for these stocks one month later? Instead of working off of only pricing data that can have many variables, you now can easily and quickly build a report and answer in depth questions with a click of a button.

The trending code is extremely easy to implement and can be used in a vast array of environments and can be universally used on all computer platforms. Every data analyst should have the trending code in their arsenal of reporting tools.

Interpretation

The trending code is as easy to interpret as it is to generate. The code can be read and used by computers and humans alike and offers a wealth of information about the data for the period that it represents.

The trending code is made up of a maximum of five digits and the code is either a positive number or a negative number. For example, say we have a trending code 37354. The first digit of this code tells the overall result of the data period. The remaining four digits show the trend of the period as shown below (Graph 1).

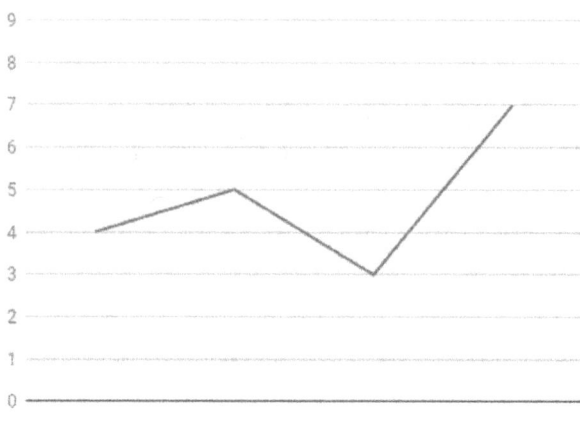

Graph 1

Notice that the trending code numbers are transposed into the graph. Without looking at the first digit, the remaining digits in the code are 7-3-5-4. Notice that on the graph, from left to right, the values are 4-5-3-7. The reason that these numbers are transposed in the trending code is that it is assumed that the value for the most current period of time is the most important value. Since it is the most important value, it needs to have a higher digit placement in the code in order to be properly queried and prioritized by the computer.

Now back to the first digit. The first digit in the trending code 37354 is the difference between the most current time period value and the oldest time period value. In this case, the difference is 7 - 4 = 3. When you look at Graph 1 it is easy to see that the value increased from 4 to 7 over the time period. This difference is how we come up with the first

4

value. It allows us to quickly find and compare other similar trending codes with great efficiency.

Let's try a different example. This time, we have trending code -62518 as shown below in graph 2. Now we know that just by looking at the first digit in the code that the during this time period the trend was a negative 6. Now we can graph the remaining four digits to find out what the trend actually looked like.

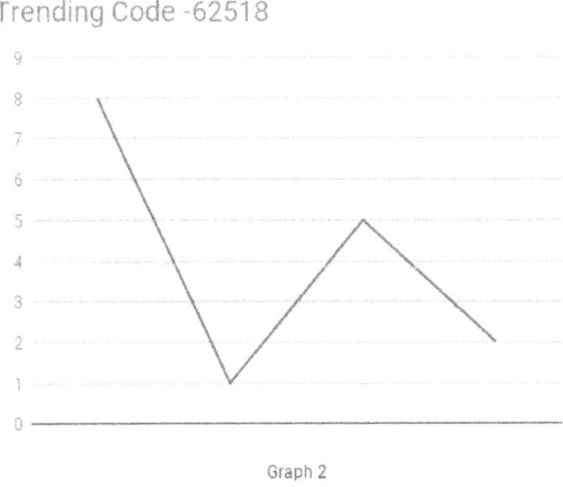

Graph 2

Right away, we can confirm that this is a downward and negative trend just like we thought by looking at the first digit. But now we can see so much more information for the time period at hand.

We can then use these trending codes to compare with other trending codes within the same dataset or to ANY other trending code available - related or unrelated. Think about all of the possibilities! Compare your company's sales trending codes to weather trending codes or stock trending codes. Compare a couple or even a thousand stock trending codes with each other. Compare trending codes produced yearly verses trending codes produced every second. By using trending codes you can find relationships between datasets that you never knew existed. These relationships will allow you to predict future trends with greater accuracy.

Creation

Trending codes are designed to be able to take any five numbers over a period of time and transform them into one five digit number. It sacrifices the overall values in order to capture a snapshot of the trend that they represent. For example, Amy's Cinnamon Rolls company sales have drastically increased over the past 20 years, so to compare current monthly sales data to data 15 years ago might seem obsolete. However, the data 15 years ago holds valuable trending information that could prove relevant even today. By using the trending codes, an analyst is able to tap into that historical information.

Creating trending codes is quick and easy and can be created once we have five numbers for a given period of time. For example, let's say Amy's Cinnamon Rolls had the following sales volume:

Month (Period)	Sales Amount
(1) January	$3,500
(2) February	$4,000
(3) March	$2,500
(4) April	$3,000
(5) May	$5,500

With this data we are able to create a trending code for the most current data in the given period of time. So for this example, the trending code would be created for the month of May.

We start by determining the highest value in the period. In this example, the highest value is $5,500. We will call this value the "Period High." Next we determine the lowest value in the period which is $2,500 for the month of March. We will call this value the "Period Low."

Now we need to calculate the total variance between the Period High and the Period Low which is formulated:

Period High - Period Low = Total Variance

$5,500 - $2,500 = $3,000 Total Variance

At this point we need to calculate the variance between each period and the Period Low. We will use these values to create a digit that we will use to fit into a five digit code.

Month (Period)	Period Value - Period Low	Period Variance
(1) January	$3,500 - $2,500	$1,000
(2) February	$4,000 - $2,500	$1,500
(3) March	$2,500 - $2,500	$0
(4) April	$3,000 - $2,500	$500
(5) May	$5,500 - $2,500	$3,000

Now we create a period variance ratio. We will use the period variance ratio in order to assign the period value a value between 0-9. This is important because in order to keep the trending code in a five digit format and to allow us to be able to read the code, all period values must be converted to single digits.

Month (Period)	Period Variance/Total Variance	Variance Ratio
(1) January	1,000 / 3,000	.33
(2) February	1,500 / 3,000	.5
(3) March	0 / 3,000	0
(4) April	500 / 3,000	.17
(5) May	3,000 / 3,000	1

Next, multiply the variance ratio by 4 and then round to the closest integer. Since the maximum variance ratio will always be 1, and 1 x 4 = 4, the maximum integer value will be four. The importance of the maximum value of four will be explained in the next step. Rounding the integer provides us with a single digit which is important for the purpose of a five digit trending code, but it also allows for more data results.

Month (Period)	Variance Ratio	Variance Integer (Ratio x 4 & rounded)
(1) January	.33	1
(2) February	.5	2
(3) March	0	0
(4) April	.17	1
(5) May	1	4

The final step is the creation of the digits of the trending code. When we create the first digit, we are displaying the overall result of the dataset. In order to do this, we need to create a digit that shows what happened over the entire period. This can be done by the following formula:

Digit 1 = (Period 5 Variance Integer - Period 1 Variance Integer + 5) - (Period 2 Variance Integer - Period 1 Variance Integer + 5)

Digit 1 = (4 - 1 + 5) - (2 - 1 + 5) = 2

Note: If digit 1 is a negative number, the entire trending code will be a negative number. If digit 1 is positive, the entire trending code will be a positive number.

In this formula, you will notice that we add five to the Period Variance Integer. This is to keep the value positive. Since the maximum value of the Variance Integer is 4, 4 + 5 = 9. 9 is the highest single digit possible and so this keeps us within the range of single digits.

Since we transpose the remaining four digits in order to allow the computer to query results based upon the assumption that the most recent period is the most relevant, we calculate the remaining digits of the trending code as follows:

Digit	Formula	Value
2	Period 5 Variance Integer - Period 1 Variance Integer + 5	8
3	Period 4 Variance Integer - Period 1 Variance Integer + 5	5
4	Period 3 Variance Integer - Period 1 Variance Integer + 5	4
5	Period 2 Variance Integer - Period 1 Variance Integer + 5	6

When you add in the first digit, the trending code is 28546 and can be displayed in graph 3.

Trending Code 28546

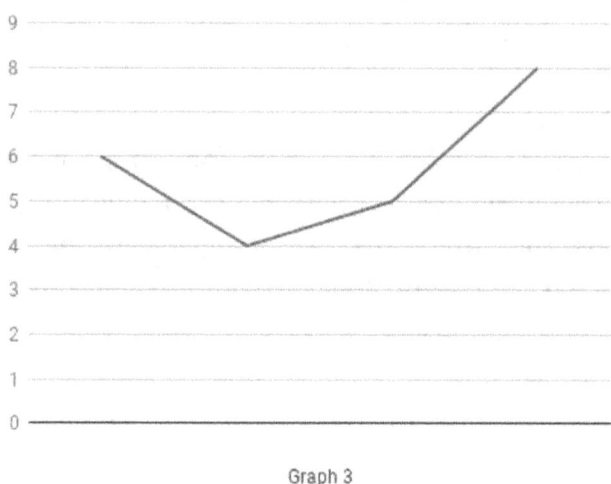

Graph 3

Now compare this trending code graph with a graph of Amy's Cinnamon Rolls original dataset.

Sales For Amy's Cinnamon Rolls

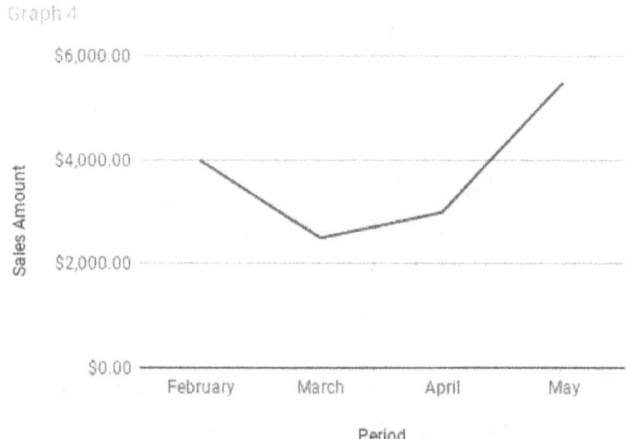

Graph 4

Notice how similar the graphs are. Just by looking at them it is easy to see that the trending code correctly captured the trend for this time period. With one code, trending data can now be calculated, compared, and analyzed across the board for *any* data captured periodically.

Utilization

The Trending Code can be used in an unlimited number of scenarios and can benefit many types of businesses, schools, churches, and non-profits. Here are a few examples:

Scenario # 1:

You trade stocks on a daily basis and analyze, research, and invest in world markets. Through researching trending codes, you have concluded that there is a relationship between four seemingly unrelated stocks. You create a program that triggers a buy option whenever this scenario occurs.

Scenario # 2:

You are an analyst for a company that sells electronics. By researching the trending codes, you are able to forecast demand for individual products with greater accuracy which allows your company to greatly reduce inventory costs while also increasing sales and customer satisfaction.

Scenario #3:

You are an analyst for an oil company and by performing data analysis on oil production you discover a relationship between oil production, earthquakes, and atmospheric conditions which allows your company to be more efficient, reduce costs, and have a large positive impact on the bottom line.

Code Example

The following trending code algorithm is programmed in Visual Basic and is illustrated for your convenience. Please fully test it for your specific application prior to implementing it into your system - specifically the error catching function, variable conversions, and the decimal rounding specifications.

```vb
Public Class TrendingClass

    Public Function TheTrendingCode(ByVal FirstVal As Decimal, ByVal
        SecondVal As Decimal, ByVal ThirdVal As Decimal, ByVal
        FourthVal As Decimal, ByVal FifthVal As Decimal) As
        Integer

    Try
        Dim PeriodHigh As Decimal = 0
        Dim PeriodLow As Decimal = 0
        Dim TotalVariance As Decimal = 0
        Dim PeriodVariance1 As Decimal = 0
        Dim PeriodVariance2 As Decimal = 0
        Dim PeriodVariance3 As Decimal = 0
        Dim PeriodVariance4 As Decimal = 0
        Dim PeriodVariance5 As Decimal = 0

        PeriodHigh = FirstVal
        If SecondVal > PeriodHigh Then PeriodHigh = SecondVal
        If ThirdVal > PeriodHigh Then PeriodHigh = ThirdVal
        If FourthVal > PeriodHigh Then PeriodHigh = FourthVal
        If FifthVal > PeriodHigh Then PeriodHigh = FifthVal

        PeriodLow = FirstVal
        If SecondVal < PeriodLow Then PeriodLow = SecondVal
        If ThirdVal < PeriodLow Then PeriodLow = ThirdVal
```

```
If FourthVal < PeriodLow Then PeriodLow = FourthVal
If FifthVal < PeriodLow Then PeriodLow = FifthVal

TotalVariance = PeriodHigh - PeriodLow

PeriodVariance1 = FirstVal - PeriodLow
PeriodVariance2 = SecondVal - PeriodLow
PeriodVariance3 = ThirdVal - PeriodLow
PeriodVariance4 = FourthVal - PeriodLow
PeriodVariance5 = FifthVal - PeriodLow

Dim PeriodVarianceRatio1 As Decimal = PeriodVariance1 /
    TotalVariance
Dim PeriodVarianceRatio2 As Decimal = PeriodVariance2 /
    TotalVariance
Dim PeriodVarianceRatio3 As Decimal = PeriodVariance3 /
    TotalVariance
Dim PeriodVarianceRatio4 As Decimal = PeriodVariance4 /
    TotalVariance
Dim PeriodVarianceRatio5 As Decimal = PeriodVariance5 /
    TotalVariance

Dim VarianceInteger1 As Integer =
    CInt(Math.Round(PeriodVarianceRatio1 * 4, 0,
    MidpointRounding.AwayFromZero))
Dim VarianceInteger2 As Integer =
    CInt(Math.Round(PeriodVarianceRatio2 * 4, 0,
    MidpointRounding.AwayFromZero))
Dim VarianceInteger3 As Integer =
    CInt(Math.Round(PeriodVarianceRatio3 * 4, 0,
    MidpointRounding.AwayFromZero))
Dim VarianceInteger4 As Integer =
    CInt(Math.Round(PeriodVarianceRatio4 * 4, 0,
    MidpointRounding.AwayFromZero))
Dim VarianceInteger5 As Integer =
    CInt(Math.Round(PeriodVarianceRatio5 * 4, 0,
    MidpointRounding.AwayFromZero))

Dim isnegative As Boolean = False
Dim digit2 As Integer = (VarianceInteger5 -
    VarianceInteger1 + 5) * 1000
Dim digit3 As Integer = (VarianceInteger4 -
    VarianceInteger1 + 5) * 100
Dim digit4 As Integer = (VarianceInteger3 -
    VarianceInteger1 + 5) * 10
Dim digit5 As Integer = VarianceInteger2 -
    VarianceInteger1 + 5

Dim digit1 As Integer = (VarianceInteger5 -
    VarianceInteger1 + 5) - (VarianceInteger2 -
    VarianceInteger1 + 5)

If digit1 < 0 Then isnegative = True
digit1 = digit1 * 10000
Dim TrendingCode As Integer = 0
If isnegative = True Then
```

```
                    digit1 = digit1 * -1
                    TrendingCode = (digit1 + digit2 + digit3 + digit4 +
                        digit5) * -1
                Else

                TrendingCode = digit1 + digit2 + digit3 + digit4 + digit5

                End If
                Return TrendingCode

            Catch ex As Exception
                Return 0
                Console.WriteLine(ex.Message)
            End Try
        End Function
End Class
```

End User License Agreement

THIS END USER LICENSE AGREEMENT ("EULA") IS A LEGAL AGREEMENT BETWEEN YOU (EITHER AN INDIVIDUAL OR AN ENTITY) AND FAIRTRAN, LLC.

Please read the following Agreement carefully.

1. Copyright & Title To The Algorithm

The algorithm as set forth in this book ("The Trending Code" by Charlie Collins), including but not limited to the calculations, processes, code, samples, any associated files and documentations (the "Trending Code algorithm"), is owned by FairTran, LLC. and is protected by copyright laws. The Trending Code algorithm and all copies, renditions, alterations, and/or modifications thereof are proprietary to FairTran, LLC. and title thereto remains in FairTran, LLC., at all times.

The Trending Code algorithm is licensed to you, not sold.

2. License

The license is for a single user and is valid for the original person for whom this book was purchased and is not transferable. The book can be purchased in either electronic or physical format, and must have been newly purchased from an authorized reseller. The single user license is NOT a 'floating' license, that is, Licensee cannot temporarily transfer access rights to another user. The single user license cannot be shared with other users. The license authorizes the single user to use the Trending Code algorithm on only one computer or device. Any other computer or user that shares the algorithm, program, or trending code information requires a new License. An additional book may be purchased in order to use the Trending Code algorithm on an additional computer or device.

3. Limited Warranty and Liability

FairTran, LLC. makes no warranties, either Express or Implied, regarding the Trending Code algorithm, including but not limited to its merchantability or its fitness for any particular purpose.

To the maximum extent permitted by law FairTran, LLC. excludes any liability for any damages, including but not limited to any loss of revenue, profit, or data, however caused, directly or indirectly, by the Trending Code algorithm or by this Agreement. **IN ANY EVENT, FairTran, LLC.'s LIABILITY FOR ANY CLAIM, WHETHER IN CONTRACT, TORT, OR ANY OTHER THEORY OF LIABILITY WILL NOT EXCEED THE GREATER OF U.S. $10.00.**

3. Usage

Usage of the Trending Code algorithm must be accompanied by a comment that reads:

"The Trending Code
Developed by Charlie Collins
www.trendingcodes.com
The following Trending Code algorithm is currently licensed."

4. Termination

If the Licensee fails to comply with any term of this Agreement, this Agreement is terminated and the Licensee has no further right to use the Trending Code algorithm. On termination, the Licensee shall have no claim on or arising from the Trending Code algorithm. The Trending Code algorithm usage shall be terminated and/or destroyed.

5. Applicable Law and Court of Jurisdiction

This Agreement is made and shall be construed in accordance with the laws of Oklahoma, United States of America. THE LICENSEE HEREBY CONSENTS AND AGREES THAT THE STATE AND/OR FEDERAL COURTS LOCATED IN THE STATE OF OKLAHOMA SHALL HAVE EXCLUSIVE JURISDICTION TO HEAR AND DETERMINE ANY CLAIMS OR DISPUTES PERTAINING TO THIS AGREEMENT.

6. Acceptance of this Agreement

By using, implementing, or testing the Trending Code algorithm, you are agreeing to this End User Licensing Agreement and agree to be bound by its terms and conditions as set forth above.

About the Author & Developer

Charlie Collins was born and raised in Oklahoma City, OK. He has a beautiful wife and seven awesome children. The question Charlie gets most often is, "How tall are you?" Charlie is 6'9" tall and he loves to coach basketball with his kids. He also loves to go to church and says that God used church to make a major impact on his life.

Charlie says, "When I figured out that I make mistakes in this life, that I'm not perfect, and that I'll never be perfect, I realized that I needed help. I needed somebody bigger than me to take away my guilt and shame. That's when I believed in Jesus Christ. That's when I was set free. That's who I live for and who I talk to every single day."

As a financial analyst for the financial and transportation sector, Charlie has a wide variety of experience with data reporting and analysis as well as computer programming. He saw the need for a better system for data research and so he developed the idea of the trending code.